P9-DOF-913

The DECLARATION of INDEPENDENCE

By John Shea

Gareth Stevens
Publishing

Please visit our website, www.garethstevens.com. For a free color catalog of all our high-quality books, call toll free 1-800-542-2595 or fax 1-877-542-2596.

Library of Congress Cataloging-in-Publication Data

Shea, John M.
The Declaration of Independence / by John M. Shea.
  p. cm. — (Documents that shaped America)
Includes index.
ISBN 978-1-4339-8998-8 (pbk.)
ISBN 9978-1-4339-8999-5 (6-pack)
ISBN 978-1-4339-8997-1 (library binding)
1. United States.—Declaration of Independence—Juvenile literature. 2. United States—Politics and government—1775-1783—Juvenile literature. I. Shea, John M. II. Title.
E221.S52 2014
973.313—d23

First Edition

Published in 2014 by
Gareth Stevens Publishing
111 East 14th Street, Suite 349
New York, NY 10003

Copyright © 2014 Gareth Stevens Publishing

Designer: Sarah Liddell
Editor: Therese Shea

Photo credits: Cover, pp. 1, 23, 27 UniversalImagesGroup/Contributor/Universal Images Group/Getty Images; p. 5 Visions of America/Contributor/Universal Images Group/Getty Images; p. 6 Getty Images/Handout/Archive Photos/Getty Images; p. 7 (King George III) Stock Montage/Contributor/Archive Photos/Getty Images;
pp. 7 (French and Indian War), 21 (Gettysburg Address) MPI/Stringer/Archive Photos/Getty Images; p. 8 Time Inc. Picture Collection/Contributor/TIME & LIFE Images/Getty Images; p. 9 DEA PICTURE LIBRARY/De Agnostini Picture Library/Getty Images; p. 11 English School/The Bridgeman Art Library/Getty Images; pp. 12, 16, 25 John Parrot/Stocktrek Images/Getty Images; p. 13 Curt Teich Postcard Archives/Contributor/Archive Photos/Getty Images; p. 14 MPI/Stringer/Hulton Royals Collection/Getty Images; p. 15 Hulton Archive/Stringer/Hulton Archive/Getty Images; p. 17 (Livingston) Stock Montage/Contributor/Archive Photos/Getty Images; p. 17 (Committee of Five) Photo Researchers/Photo Researchers/Getty Images; p. 18 After Alonzo Chappel/The Bridgeman Art Library/Getty Images; p. 19 Richard Nowitz/National Geographic/Getty Images;
p. 20 photo courtesy of Wikimedia Commons, Declaration of the Rights of Man and of the Citizen in 1789.jpg; p. 21 (Lincoln) Archive/Stringer/Archive Photos/Getty Images;
p. 28 Todd Gipstein/National Geographic/Getty Images.

All rights reserved. No part of this book may be reproduced in any form without permission in writing from the publisher, except by a reviewer.

Printed in the United States of America

CPSIA compliance information: Batch #CS13GS: For further information contact Gareth Stevens, New York, New York at 1-800-542-2595.

CONTENTS

Words in the glossary appear in **bold** type the first time they are used in the text.

"WHEN IN THE COURSE of HUMAN EVENTS"

From the time the first British settlers arrived in Jamestown, Virginia, in 1607, England governed colonies in North America. The relationship between the American colonies and England was friendly for more than 100 years. The British government rarely interfered in the daily lives of colonists. They allowed the colonies' governing bodies to make most laws. The colonists were only taxed on British goods. (However, because colonists weren't supposed to trade with other countries, many colonial **smugglers** secretly transported goods in and out.)

Meanwhile, the British army and navy protected American lands and ships. Despite the thousands of miles separating the two lands, before 1770, most American colonists still proudly considered themselves British citizens.

It's a Fact!

During the War of 1812 (1812–1815), the Declaration of Independence was moved to a house in Virginia to protect it from the British. During World War II (1939–1945), it was stored at Fort Knox in Kentucky.

The original signed copy of the Declaration of Independence is on display under armed guard at the National Archives in Washington, DC. At night, it's stored in a bombproof vault.

READ ALONG

The chapter titles in this book are quotes from one of the most important **documents** in American and world history. The first half of this book describes the events that led to the writing of the Declaration of Independence, while the second half examines the document's contents. You can read the Declaration of Independence along with this book. It can be found on the US National Archives' website: www.archives.gov/exhibits/charters/declaration.html

"THE CAUSES . . . TO THE SEPARATION"

The relationship between England and the American colonies became strained during the French and Indian War. Between 1756 and 1763, the British and French battled for control of vast areas of North America.

Many colonists didn't care about the war, thinking it was England's conflict, not theirs. Others wanted to be able to defend their lands from the French. They asked for the British government's permission to raise an American army. The king of England, suspicious of their motives, wouldn't allow it. Colonists were asked to fight with the British army, and thousands did. However, many were kept from holding high-ranking positions, insulted, and sometimes even sent home by British officers. Colonists began to question what it meant to be a British citizen in America.

It's a Fact!

George Washington fought in the French and Indian War. His military experience helped him lead the American forces in the war for independence.

George Washington

THE BRITISH MILITARY

During the time leading up to the American Revolution, the British army was among the best in the world. Likewise, the British navy was the strongest force on the oceans. Both the British army and navy were well funded by the British government. Some of those funds went to hiring extra support for the army. German soldiers for hire, called Hessians, fought with the British against the Americans in the American Revolution.

King George III

7

The French and Indian War was an expensive conflict, and the British thought the American colonies should help pay for it. In 1764, the British introduced the Sugar Act, which placed a tax on sugar, molasses, and other goods. The following year, England passed the Stamp Act, which taxed paper goods, including newspapers, playing cards, and legal documents. Other taxes followed.

To help patrol the land won from the French, the British kept a large number of soldiers in North America after the war. The Quartering Act of 1765 stated that colonists had to provide food, shelter, and supplies to the British forces. The presence of so many soldiers in their cities and towns made many American colonists tense.

An Emblem of the Effects of the STAMP
O! the fatal Stamp

It's a Fact!

England's **debt** almost doubled from 1755 to 1764. British citizens in England were so heavily taxed the government was concerned they might rise up against it.

The presence of British soldiers in colonial cities and towns created a lot of tension. On March 5, 1770, a conflict between British soldiers and Americans resulted in the deaths of five colonists. The event was called the Boston Massacre.

SHAPING A NATION

Many of the events that occurred in the decade before the American Revolution shaped how the Founding Fathers viewed important rights and freedoms. For example, the Third Amendment of the Bill of Rights bans the peacetime quartering, or housing, of soldiers in someone's house without the owner's permission. In wartime, quartering would require special laws. This protection is a direct result of the Quartering Act of 1765.

"THE RIGHT of REPRESENTATION"

The freedoms colonists had enjoyed before the French and Indian War disappeared after 1763. The British government became a constant presence in their lives. Many colonists weren't just angry about how costly taxes were, but also that these laws had been passed thousands of miles away without regard to colonists' opinions. "No taxation without representation" became a rallying cry among the protestors.

The British response was to take more control over the American colonies. When the New York colonial assembly voted not to obey the Quartering Act, the British disbanded, or broke up, the assembly. After colonists dumped tea into Boston Harbor to protest **restrictions** on the tea trade, King George III limited the powers of the government of Massachusetts as well.

It's a Fact!

Samuel Adams, cousin of John Adams, was one of the first colonists to publicly support independence from England in 1765. In 1776, he signed the Declaration of Independence, and he was elected governor of Massachusetts in 1794.

The Tea Act of 1773 forced American colonists to buy tea from only one British company. In protest, colonists dressed as Native Americans dumped 342 crates of tea into Boston Harbor.

THE DAUGHTERS OF LIBERTY

In response to increasing taxes on imported goods, groups of women in the colonies helped organize **boycotts** in protest. Instead of buying British goods, the Daughters of Liberty made their own, such as cloth and clothing. Their hard work allowed the American colonies to be less dependent on goods imported from England. This helped the First Continental Congress decide to officially boycott all British goods in 1774.

"TO DISSOLVE POLITICAL BANDS"

The actions King George III took to punish the colonies of New York and Massachusetts were meant to discourage other colonies from disobeying British authorities. However, they had the opposite effect; other colonies felt sympathy for New York and Massachusetts and became angry with the British government. In September 1774, representatives from every American colony except Georgia formed the First Continental Congress to discuss what to do next.

In October 1774, the Congress sent a letter to King George III stating their **grievances**. The representatives explained that they weren't asking for special rights but were seeking fair and equal treatment. Importantly, the letter clearly stated that the colonists were loyal to the king.

It's a Fact!

At age 70, Benjamin Franklin was the oldest person to sign the Declaration of Independence. Edward Rutledge of South Carolina was the youngest at 26 years old.

Benjamin Franklin

Carpenters' Hall remains one of the most historic buildings in the United States. Besides hosting the First Continental Congress, it was home to the First and Second Banks of the United States as well as Benjamin Franklin's Library Company.

FIRST CONTINENTAL CONGRESS

The First Continental Congress met in Carpenters' Hall in Philadelphia, Pennsylvania, between September 5 and October 26, 1774. The purpose of the Congress was to show a united stand in dealing with England, but in truth, the colonies weren't united at all. Some wanted peace with England, others wanted more colonial rights, and still other colonies wanted complete separation. They did agree that the first step was to inform the king of the colonies' concerns.

Tensions continued to rise in the colonies, especially after the Battles of Lexington and Concord in April 1775. The Second Continental Congress met in Philadelphia in May 1775. This Congress prepared for the worst: war with England. They formed the Continental army and appointed George Washington as its general.

However, many of the delegates still hoped for peace. In July 1775, they wrote the Olive Branch **Petition**, which pleaded with King George III to stop taking action against the colonies. Again, the Congress emphasized the colonies' loyalty to their king.

King George refused to read the Olive Branch Petition. When news of this rejection reached the colonies, it changed the opinion of many Americans. They began to see King George as a tyrant.

Olive Branch Petition ←

To the King's Most Excellent Majesty.

Most Gracious Sovereign!

We your Majesty's faithful Subjects of the colonies of New-Hampshire, Massachusetts-Bay, Rhode-Island and Providence Plantations, Connecticut, New-York, New-Jersey, Pensylvania, the Counties of New-Castle, Delaware, Maryland, Virginia, in behalf of ourselves and the have deputed us to represent them in our humble petition, beg leave to the throne.

A standing army has been kept in the conclusion of the late war, without assemblies, and this army with a considerable has been employed to enforce the collection of taxes

It's a Fact!

Part of the British plan during the march to Concord, Massachusetts, in 1775 was to arrest Samuel Adams and John Hancock. Paul Revere's famous "midnight ride" successfully warned the two leaders.

The opening days of the American Revolution were fought without an organized American army. Instead, militia clashed with the British. They were nicknamed "minutemen" for how quickly they could get ready to fight.

THE BATTLES OF LEXINGTON AND CONCORD

Fought on April 19, 1775, the Battles of Lexington and Concord started the American Revolution. British officers marched from Boston to Concord, Massachusetts, to capture colonial weapon supplies. **Militia** confronted the British soldiers in nearby Lexington. To this day, no one knows which side fired the first shot of the war. Although they were outnumbered at first, several hundred colonists joined the battle and forced the most powerful army in the world to retreat.

"TO INSTITUTE NEW GOVERNMENT"

American attitudes had shifted greatly in a few short years. Many of those who were once loyal to the king openly called for independence. On June 7, 1776, Virginia delegate Richard Henry Lee proposed "that these United Colonies are, and of right ought to be, free and independent States." The Continental Congress needed a document that would present the reasons for independence to American colonists, England, and the world.

A Committee of Five (Roger Sherman, Robert Livingston, John Adams, Benjamin Franklin, and Thomas Jefferson) was selected to write this document. Jefferson wrote most of it, with Adams and Franklin suggesting a few changes. Jefferson included in this Declaration of Independence the specific grievances the colonies had with British rule.

It's a Fact!

Thomas Jefferson was an early supporter of American independence. In 1774, he wrote "A Summary View of the Rights of British America," which gained him a reputation as a powerful writer.

Thomas Jefferson

FOUNDING FATHER ROBERT LIVINGSTON

Although Robert Livingston was on the committee to write the Declaration, he was called back to his home state of New York before he could sign it. He was later named the US secretary of foreign affairs and was a delegate to the New York assembly to approve the US Constitution in 1788. Livingston gave the presidential oath of office to George Washington in 1789. In 1803, he helped complete the **Louisiana Purchase** with France.

Robert Livingston

Besides writing most of the Declaration of Independence, Thomas Jefferson was the nation's first US secretary of state, the second vice president, and the third president.

"IT BECOMES NECESSARY"

The Declaration of Independence is composed of three main parts: a preamble, a list of grievances, and a formal statement declaring independence.

Jefferson began: "When in the course of human events, it becomes necessary for one people to **dissolve** the political bands which have connected them with another . . .". He was making powerful arguments for independence with these words. Jefferson was proposing that not only should Americans have independence, it was "necessary" for them. He identified Americans as "one people" and the British as "another." In doing so, Jefferson was suggesting that the colonists weren't British citizens anymore. This was important to other countries that wouldn't want to get involved in a British **civil war**.

Thomas Jefferson

It's a Fact!

Thomas Jefferson wrote the Declaration of Independence in about 3 weeks in a house in Philadelphia. The house was torn down in 1883, but was rebuilt and renamed the Declaration House in 1975.

VIRGINIA DECLARATION OF RIGHTS

Some of Jefferson's ideas in the Preamble of the Declaration of Independence were influenced by an important document from his home state: the Virginia Declaration of Rights. Written by George Mason in 1776, the Declaration of Rights had many themes similar to the Declaration of Independence, such as the belief that all men have freedoms that cannot be taken away, including the rights to life, liberty, and the pursuit of happiness.

A preamble is a piece of writing that introduces the purpose of a document. The Preamble of the Declaration of Independence has become the most famous part.

"THAT ALL MEN ARE CREATED EQUAL"

In the Preamble, Jefferson maintained that "all men are created equal" with "**unalienable**" rights that can't be taken away. He stated that it's the job of the government to protect those rights, and the power of the government comes from the people. If the government abuses that power, Jefferson argued, then it's the right and duty of citizens to overthrow that government and establish a new, just one.

These ideas not only signaled a change in the course of American history, they later helped spark cries for independence around the world, including in the Netherlands, Venezuela, and Mexican-controlled Texas. In each of these places, the new nations wrote their own declarations of independence using words and phrases similar to the American document.

It's a Fact!

The French "Declaration of the Rights of Man and the Citizen" was inspired by the Declaration of Independence. Written in 1789, the French Declaration states that men have "natural, unalienable and sacred rights."

Declaration of the Rights of Man and the Citizen

Abraham Lincoln gave his Gettysburg Address on November 19, 1863, at the dedication of the Soldiers' National Cemetery in Gettysburg, Pennsylvania.

GETTYSBURG ADDRESS

One of the most famous documents in American history inspired one of its most well-known speeches. "Four score and 7 years" (87 years) after the signing of the Declaration of Independence, Abraham Lincoln referred to the Founding Fathers' idea that "all men are created equal." Lincoln stated the American Civil War (1861–1865) would result in "a new birth of freedom," not just for white Americans, but for everyone.

21

"A HISTORY of REPEATED INJURIES"

Jefferson argued in the Preamble that citizens have a duty to overthrow an unjust government. In the middle section, which makes up about two-thirds of the text, the Declaration lists ways the British government mistreated the colonists.

Twenty-eight examples are given, including the king's interference with colonial governments and his army's occupation of colonial land during peacetime. Jefferson also listed taxation without consent, the prevention of trade with other countries, and disregard for the colonists' right to trial by jury. The Declaration accused the British ruler of waging a war on his own colonies.

Jefferson concluded the grievances by pointing out that while King George III was abusing the rights of the colonists, the British government and people didn't protest. This was another reason why the colonists wanted to separate from them.

It's a Fact!

In an early version of the Declaration, Jefferson condemned King George III for allowing slavery, calling it "a cruel war against human nature"—even though Jefferson himself was a slave owner. However, some delegates insisted that grievance be removed.

JUST THE FACTS

Jefferson began the list of grievances with the shortest sentence in the Declaration: "To prove this, let Facts be submitted to a **candid** world." Jefferson called his points "facts," not disagreements or opinions. This sentence also reveals the audience for the document. The Continental Congress was announcing the colonies' right of independence not just to Americans or the British government, but to the world.

"FULL POWER TO LEVY WAR"

The second part of the Declaration of Independence states the many actions the British king was guilty of in the eyes of the delegates. The third and final section says what the colonists wanted to do about it: "These United Colonies are, and of Right ought to be Free and Independent States."

Several important points are made in this section. First, the Declaration broke all ties with the British government. Next, the colonies asserted they had the right to levy, or wage, war and declare peace. Third, the document established that the new United States could form **alliances** with other countries. Finally, the Americans declared that they had "full Power . . . to do all other Acts and Things which Independent States may of right do."

It's a Fact!

The name "United States of America" was first used in the Declaration of Independence.

Benjamin Franklin, who helped
Jefferson write the Declaration,
was important in gathering French
support for the colonies during the
American Revolution. He's shown
here at the French court.

ALLIANCES

The Declaration helped the United States form alliances during the
American Revolution. The British had defeated the French in the
French and Indian War, so France looked favorably on the colonies'
actions against its enemy. France came to the United States' aid in
1778. In addition, the United States borrowed money for the war
from Spain in 1779. It would have been very hard for the United
States to win independence without outside help.

"THE UNITED STATES of AMERICA"

On July 2, 1776, the Second Continental Congress finally accepted Richard Henry Lee's proposal for independence. While a majority of the colonies needed to agree for this proposal to pass (7 out of 13), Congress thought it was important that the colonies appear united. Twelve out of 13 colonies voted for independence, and New York agreed a few days later.

Congress then considered the Declaration of Independence. They liked most of the document but thought some words should change. A total of 86 changes were made to Jefferson's original version, but the core ideas and phrases remained. The edited Declaration of Independence was presented to Congress. On July 4, 1776, this historic document was officially adopted by the new American government.

It's a Fact!

Thomas Jefferson and John Adams both died on July 4, 1826, exactly 50 years after the approval of the Declaration.

THE REAL INDEPENDENCE DAY?

Although Americans celebrate Independence Day on July 4, perhaps the United States' real birthday should be the day when the Second Continental Congress voted for independence: July 2. John Adams predicted in a letter to his wife, Abigail, that July 2 would be celebrated for years to come. But a year later, Philadelphia marked Independence Day on July 4, 1777, by celebrating with fires, bells, and fireworks. Congress established Independence Day as a holiday in 1870.

Although John Adams was wrong about the date of the holiday, he was correct that Americans would celebrate their independence with parades, games, and lights, even centuries later.

"OUR LIVES, OUR FORTUNES, AND OUR SACRED HONOR"

The Declaration of Independence wasn't signed until about a month after its approval. Part of this delay was because Congress was waiting for the Declaration to be "engrossed," or written clearly on parchment paper. On August 2, 1776, most of the delegates signed the Declaration. They knew they were putting their lives in danger, but they believed it was the honorable thing to do.

The American Revolution lasted another 7 years after the Declaration was signed, and the cost was many American lives. Even after the war, the United States faced many tests, including a new government and a civil war. Throughout these challenges, the principles of the Declaration—including equality, unalienable rights, and a just government—remained an important cornerstone of the nation.

John Hancock

John Hancock, president of the Second Continental Congress, was the first to sign the Declaration on August 2, 1776. His large, bold signature is one of the most famous signatures in American history.

It's a Fact!

George Washington read the Declaration of Independence aloud to a crowd in New York City. The excited crowd tore down a statue of King George III, melted it, and made **ammunition** out of it!

DECLARATION of INDEPENDENCE TIMELINE

1763
French and Indian War ends

1774
First Continental Congress meets

1778
France becomes a US ally

1765
England passes the Stamp Act and the Quartering Act

1776
Declaration of Independence is written and approved

1756
French and Indian War begins

1764
England passes the Sugar Act

1773
England passes Tea Act; tea dumped into Boston Harbor

1775
Second Continental Congress meets

1770
Boston Massacre occurs

1783
Treaty of Paris is signed, ending the American Revolution

1760
George III becomes king of England

1775
American Revolution begins

DUNLAP BROADSIDES

Immediately after approval of the Declaration of Independence, Congress asked Philadelphia printer John Dunlap to print about 200 copies. These copies, known as broadsides, were sent throughout the states and given to local leaders, newspapers, and soldiers fighting the war. One of these copies was sent to England as the United States' official announcement of their independence. Only 26 of the Dunlap broadsides remain today. One sold for $8 million in 2000!

GLOSSARY

alliance: an agreement between two or more people or countries to work together

ammunition: bullets, shells, and other things fired by weapons

boycott: the act of refusing to have dealings with a person or business in order to force change

candid: open, sincere, and fair

civil war: a war between two groups within a country

debt: an amount of money owed

dissolve: to bring to an end

document: a formal piece of writing

grievance: complaint

Louisiana Purchase: territory of the western United States bought from France in 1803

militia: a group of people who only fight when needed

petition: a written request signed by many people asking the government to take an action

restriction: something that limits or controls

smuggler: one who imports or exports goods illegally

unalienable: not capable of being taken away

FOR MORE INFORMATION

BOOKS

Isaacs, Sally Senzell. *Understanding the Declaration of Independence.* New York, NY: Crabtree Publishing Company, 2009.

McDaniel, Melissa. *The Declaration of Independence.* New York, NY: Children's Press, 2012.

Raum, Elizabeth. *The Declaration of Independence.* Chicago, IL: Heinemann Library, 2013.

WEBSITES

The Declaration of Independence
www.ushistory.org/declaration/
Run by the Independence Hall Association of Philadelphia, this website has many facts about the Declaration of Independence and the American Revolution.

National Archives and Records Administration
www.archives.gov
The National Archives website contains a collection of historical documents for easy access, including the Declaration of Independence.

Publisher's note to educators and parents: Our editors have carefully reviewed these websites to ensure that they are suitable for students. Many websites change frequently, however, and we cannot guarantee that a site's future contents will continue to meet our high standards of quality and educational value. Be advised that students should be closely supervised whenever they access the Internet.

INDEX

DISCARD

J 973.3 SHEA

Shea, John M.
The Declaration of
Independence

METRO

R4001373139

METROPOLITAN
Atlanta-Fulton Public Library